Level 3 Manageme Accounting: Costing

Practice Assessment 1

By

Teresa Clarke FMAAT

This practice assessment has been designed and written to be like the real AAT Level 3 Management Accounting: Costing exam. It includes a similar mark scheme so you can work out your percentage pass rate too.

Answers are shown on page 17 onwards. A marks sheet is included at the back of this assessment for you to record your marks. You need 70% to pass this exam.

NOTE:

Unlike other practice assessments, I have shown workings and given explanations to help you understand the answers. This will help you to understand any errors you make.

Time allowed – 2 hours 30 minutes

Task 1: (16 marks)

Date of Purchase	Number of Units	Cost per Unit £	Total Cost £
1 January	150	3.00	450
8 January	120	2.00	240
12 January	200	2.50	500

An issue was made on 15 January of 350 units.

Complete the table below.

	Cost
FIFO issue	
LIFO issue	
AVCO issue	
FIFO balance	
LIFO balance	
AVCO balance	

Workings:

Task 2: (16 marks)

Michelle uses the following codes in her accounting system.

Ledger	Code
Bank	5000
Stores	6000
Maintenance	7000
Purchase Ledger Control Account	8000
Production	9000

Using these codes complete the tables below.

a) A payment of £2000 to a supplier for some materials purchased on credit. (4 marks)

	Code	£
Debit		
Credit		

b) Materials to the value of £350 are returned to the stores from the maintenance department. (4 marks)

	Code	£
Debit		
Credit		

c) Issue of 200 units at £1.50 each from stores to the production department. (4 marks)

	Code	£
Debit		
Credit		

d) Return of 32 units at £1.50 each from production to stores. (4 marks)

	Code	£
Debit		
Credit		

Task 3: (12 marks)

A team of packers in a manufacturing plant are paid a basic wage of £300 each for a 35-hour week.

For every hour above that, they are paid an overtime rate of £10 per hour.

They are expected to pack 10 boxes for every hour they work.

A bonus of £2 per box is paid for any boxes in excess of the expected level.

There are 5 people in the packing team.

They have packed 2,250 boxes.

They have worked a total of 186 hours this week.

a) Complete the following table for the team. (10 marks)

Labour cost	Hours worked	Amount due £
Basic pay		
Overtime pay		
Bonus pay		
Total wages payable to team		

b) Calculate the average labour rate per hour for the packing department this week. Round your answer to the nearest whole £. (2 marks)

Task 4: (18 marks)

Garden Chairs R Us Ltd manufacture garden chairs from their factory in Kings Lynn. They have four cost centres, of which two are service cost centres and two are production cost centres.

Cost Centres:

Service Cost Centres:	Warehouse and Storage
	Selling and Distribution
Production Cost Centres:	Assembly Department
	Finishing Department

Garden Chairs R Us Ltd has the following budgeted overheads for the year ahead:

Rent of buildings	£8,000
Insurance of buildings	£1,600
Insurance of machinery	£2,200
Machinery depreciation	£8,600
Electricity	£4,200
Cleaning for the whole premises	£7,500
Warehouse and storage costs	£9,400

Information about the cost centres:

Basis	Assembly Dept.	Finishing Dept.	Warehouse and Storage	Selling and Distribution
Floor area m²	300	200	350	150
Carrying value of machinery £	800,000	700,000	0	0
Number of employees	10	15	5	10
Material requisitions from warehouse	600	900	0	0

Complete the table below, allocating and apportioning the overheads over all four cost centres. Then re-apportion the service centre costs to the production centres.

Warehouse costs should be re-apportioned based on material requisitions. Selling and distribution costs should to re-apportioned equally between the two production centres.

Round your answers to the nearest whole £.

Overhead	Basis of allocation or apportionment £	Total £	Assembly Dept. £	Finishing Dept. £	Warehouse and Storage £	Selling and Distribution £
Rent of buildings						
Insurance of buildings						
Insurance of machinery						
Machinery depreciation						
Electricity						
Cleaning of whole premises						
Warehouse and storage costs						
Total						
Re-apportionment: Warehouse and storage						
Re-apportionment: Selling and distribution						
Total						

Task 5: (15 marks)

You have been provided with the following budgeted information.

	Department Muddle £	Department Huddle £
Budgeted Overheads	450,000	520,000
Actual Overheads	433,000	515,000
Budgeted Labour Hours	2,250	840
Actual Labour Hours	2,330	780
Budgeted Machine Hours	420	1,250
Actual Machine Hours	425	1,120

a) Calculate the budgeted overhead absorption rate for Department Muddle using labour hours, and for Department Huddle using machine hours. (7 marks)

	Department Muddle £	Department Huddle £
Budgeted overhead absorption rate OAR		

b) Calculate the over or under absorption for each department. (7 marks)

	Overheads incurred £	Overheads absorbed £	Difference £	Under/over absorption
Department Muddle				*Under / Over absorption*
Department Huddle				*Under / Over absorption*

c) An under absorption of overheads will be *debited / credited* to the Statement of Profit or Loss. (delete as appropriate) (1 mark)

Task 6: (25 marks)

a) Using the following information, complete the table below to calculate the profit of the planned production of each product. Round your answers to the nearest whole £. (20 marks)

Budgeted units for Product AB1 are 5,000 units.

Budgeted units for Product AC2 are 25% more than AB1 and budgeted units for Product AD3 is 10% more than AC2.

The sale price per unit of AB1 is £6. The sale price of AC2 is 15% more than AB1. The sale price of AD3 is 20% more than AC2.

Variable costs per unit of AB1 is £1. Variable costs per unit for AC2 and AD3 is 10% more than AB1.

Fixed costs of £1,800 are to be shared between AB1, AC2 and AD3 in the ratio of 3:2:1.

	Product AB1	Product AC2	Product AD3
Budgeted units			
Sales revenue £			
Variable costs £			
Contribution £			
Fixed costs £			
Profit £			

b) Your friend works for a rival company and has asked for details about this budget. Do you release this information? Explain your answer. (5 marks)

....

....

....

....

....

....

....

....

....

Task 7: (16 marks)

Using the information below, complete the table to calculate the total products we can produce based on the limiting factor.

Product	Total labour hours	Budgeted production levels	Total contribution £
Rum Tum	125	250	750
Bing Bong	225	300	630
Lim Lam	120	200	640

Total fixed costs are £900, and this is to be shared equally between the product ranges.

Due to Covid, we have a limited number of production staff available, so the total labour hours available is 400.

Complete the table below. Round your answers to two decimal places.

	Rum Tum	Bing Bong	Lim Lam	Total
Contribution per unit £				
Contribution per labour hour £				
Ranking				
Total labour hours available				
Labour hours allocated				
Units to produce				
Total contribution				
Less fixed costs				
Profit				

Task 8: (16 marks)

Identify the correct cost classification for each of the following. Choose from *fixed, variable, semi-variable and stepped.*

a) Cost classification 1: (4 marks)

Units	Cost per unit
2,000	£16.00
3,000	£14.00
5,000	£12.40
8,000	£11.50

Cost classification – *fixed / variable / semi-variable / stepped*

b) Calculate the total cost for 10,000 units. (4 marks)

c) Cost classification 2: (4 marks)

Units	Total cost
2,000	£18,000
3,000	£27,000
5,000	£45,000
8,000	£72,000

Cost classification – *fixed / variable / semi-variable / stepped*

d) Calculate the total cost for 10,000 units. (4 marks)

Task 9: (16 marks)

a) You have been asked to prepare the flexed budget and then compare your new budget with the actual results. Complete the following table. (12 marks)

Adverse variances should be shown with a minus sign or brackets.

Round your answers to the nearest whole £.

	Budget	Flexed Budget	Actual	Variance
Units	60,000	56,000	56,000	
	£	£	£	£
Sales revenue	1,380,000	1,288,000	1,340,000	52,000
Less costs				
Manufacturing costs	252,000	235,200	230,000	5,200
Delivery costs	180,000	168,000	172,000	(4,000)
Fixed overheads	138,000	138,000	130,500	7,500
Profit	810,000	746,800	807,500	60,700

b) Explain a possible reason for the sales revenue variance. (4 marks)

....

....

Task 10: (20 marks)

The following information has been received and you have been asked to comment on the proposals:

Appraisal	Notes	Company Policy	Project Results
Payback Period		Accept if 3.5 years or less	4 years
Net Present Value NPV	Discount at 12% cost of capital	Accept if positive	£30,000 +
Internal Rate of Return	Discount at 12% cost of capital	Must exceed cost of capital	11%

Evaluate this information and suggest to the manager whether to accept the proposed project.

Appraisal method	Recommendation
Payback period	Reject as payback period is longer than company policy. Or Accept as payback period is longer than company policy.
NPV	Reject as NPV is positive. Or Accept as NPV is positive
IRR	Accept as IRR exceeds the cost of capital. Or Reject as IRR does not exceed the cost of capital.
Overall	Accept based on the most important criteria. Or Reject based on the most important criteria.

Answers

Answers are shown in bold.

Workings and explanations are included to help you understand the answers.

Task 1: (16 marks) answers

Date of Purchase	Number of Units	Cost per Unit £	Total Cost £
1 January	150	3.00	450
8 January	120	2.00	240
12 January	200	2.50	500

An issue was made on 15 January of 350 units.

Complete the table below. (Round your answers to the nearest whole £)

	Cost
FIFO issue	**£890**
LIFO issue	**£830**
AVCO issue	**£886**
FIFO balance	**£300**
LIFO balance	**£360**
AVCO balance	**£304**

Workings:
FIFO: 1 Jan 150 units + 8 Jan 120 units + 12 Jan 80 units = 350 units
£450 + £240 + (£2.50 x 80 units) = £890
LIFO: 12 Jan 200 units + 8 Jan 120 units + 1 Jan 30 units = 350 units
£500 + £240 + (£3.00 x 30 units) = £830
AVCO: (£450 + 240 + £500) ÷ (150 units + 120 units + 200 units) =
£1,190 ÷ 470 units = 2.531914 (leave that in your calculator) x the issue of
350 units = £886 (rounded to the nearest whole £)

Balances: Total cost less issue.
FIFO: £1,190 - £890 (taken from your previous answer) = £300
LIFO: £1,190 - £830 = £360
AVCO: £1,190 - £886 = £304

Task 2: (16 marks) answers

Michelle uses the following codes in her accounting system.

Ledger	Code
Bank	5000
Stores	6000
Maintenance	7000
Purchase Ledger Control Account	8000
Production	9000

Using these codes complete the tables below.

a) A payment of £2000 to a supplier for some materials purchased on credit. (4 marks)

	Code	£
Debit	**8000**	**2000**
Credit	**5000**	**2000**

Explanation: The payment came out of the bank as a credit and paid to a credit supplier, so debited in the PLCA.

b) Materials to the value of £350 are returned to the stores from the maintenance department. (4 marks)

	Code	£
Debit	**6000**	**350**
Credit	**7000**	**350**

Explanation: The goods were returned from the maintenance department, so credited from that code. The goods were returned to the stores so debited to that code.

c) Issue of 200 units at £1.50 each from stores to the production department. (4 marks)

	Code	£
Debit	9000	300
Credit	6000	300

Explanation: The issue came from the stores department, so this was credited. The goods went to the production department, so this was debited. The value of the issue was 200 units x £1.50.

d) Return of 32 units at £1.50 each from production to stores. (4 marks)

	Code	£
Debit	6000	48
Credit	9000	48

Explanation: The return came from production, so this was credited. The goods went back to the stores department, so this was debited. The value of the return was 32 units x £1.50.

Task 3: (12 marks) answers

A team of packers in a manufacturing plant are paid a basic wage of £300 each for a 35-hour week.

For every hour above that, they are paid an overtime rate of £10 per hour.

They are expected to pack 10 boxes for every hour they work.

A bonus of £2 per box is paid for any boxes in excess of the expected level.

There are 5 people in the packing team.

They have packed 2,250 boxes.

They have worked a total of 186 hours this week.

a) Complete the following table for the team. (10 marks)

Labour cost	Hours worked	Amount due £
Basic pay	**175** **(5 packers x 35 hours each)**	**1,500** **(£300 basic wage x 5 packers)**
Overtime pay	**11** **(Total hours worked of 186 less basic pay hours of 175)**	**110** **(11 hours x overtime rate of £10 per hour)**
Bonus pay		**780** **(Expected to pack 10 boxes per hour so 10 x 186 hours = 1,860 boxes. Actually packed 2,250 boxes, so 390 in excess of expected level. 390 boxes x £2 bonus rate)**
Total wages payable to team		**2,390** **(1,500 + 110 + 780)**

b) Calculate the average labour rate per hour for the packing department this week. Round your answer to the nearest whole £. (2 marks)

£12.85
£2,390 (total labour cost) ÷ 186 hours (total hours worked)

Task 4: (18 marks) answers

Garden Chairs R Us Ltd manufacture garden chairs from their factory in Kings Lynn. They have four cost centres, of which two are service cost centres and two are production cost centres.

Cost Centres:

Service Cost Centres:	Warehouse and Storage
	Selling and Distribution
Production Cost Centres:	Assembly Department
	Finishing Department

Garden Chairs R Us Ltd has the following budgeted overheads for the year ahead:

Rent of buildings	£8,000
Insurance of buildings	£1,600
Insurance of machinery	£2,200
Machinery depreciation	£8,600
Electricity	£4,200
Cleaning for the whole premises	£7,500
Warehouse and storage costs	£9,400

Information about the cost centres:

Basis	Assembly Dept.	Finishing Dept.	Warehouse and Storage	Selling and Distribution
Floor area m²	300	200	350	150
Carrying value of machinery £	800,000	700,000	0	0
Number of Employees	10	15	5	10
Material requisitions from warehouse	600	900	0	0

Complete the table below, allocating and apportioning the overheads over all four cost centres. Then re-apportion the service centre costs to the production centres.

Warehouse costs should be re-apportioned based on material requisitions. Selling and distribution costs should to re-apportioned equally between the two production centres.

Round your answers to the nearest whole £.

Overhead	Basis of allocation or apportion-ment	Total £	Assembly Dept. £	Finishing Dept. £	Warehouse and Storage £	Selling and Distribution £
Rent of buildings	**Floor area**	8,000	2,400 (total costs ÷ total floor area) x floor area of assembly dept (£8,000 ÷ 1000 sq m) x 300 = 2,400	1,600 (total costs ÷ total floor area) x floor area of finishing dept (£8,000 ÷ 1000 sq m) x 200 = 1,600	2,800 (total costs ÷ total floor area) x floor area of warehouse & storage dept (£8,000 ÷ 1000 sq m) x 350 = 2,800	1,200 (total costs ÷ total floor area) x floor area of selling & distribution dept (£8,000 ÷ 1000 sq m) x 150 = 1,200
Insurance of buildings	**Floor area**	1,600	480 (total costs ÷ total floor area) x floor area of assembly dept (£1,600 ÷ 1000 sq m) x 300 = 480	320 (total costs ÷ total floor area) x floor area of finishing dept (£1,600 ÷ 1000 sq m) x 200 = 320	560 (total costs ÷ total floor area) x floor area of warehouse & storage dept (£1,600 ÷ 1000 sq m) x 350 = 560	240 (total costs ÷ total floor area) x floor area of selling & distribution dept (£1,600 ÷ 1000 sq m) x 150 = 240
Insurance of machinery	**Carrying value of machinery**	2,200	1,173 (total costs ÷ total carrying value of machinery) x carrying value of assembly dept machinery (£2,200 ÷ 1,500,000) x 800,000 = 1,173 (rounded)	1,027 (total costs ÷ total carrying value of machinery) x carrying value of finishing dept machinery (£2,200 ÷ 1,500,000) x 700,000 = 1,027 (rounded)		
Machinery depreciation	**Carrying value of machinery**	8,600	4,587 (total costs ÷ total carrying value of machinery) x carrying value of assembly dept machinery (£8,600 ÷ 1,500,000) x 800,000 = 4,587 (rounded)	4,013 (total costs ÷ total carrying value of machinery) x carrying value of finishing dept machinery (£8,600 ÷ 1,500,000) x 700,000 = 4,013 (rounded)		

		Total	Assembly	Finishing	Warehouse & storage	Selling & distribution
Electricity	**Floor area**	4,200	**1,260** (total costs ÷ total floor area) x floor area of assembly dept (£4,200 ÷ 1000 sq m) x 300 = 1,260	**840** (total costs ÷ total floor area) x floor area of finishing dept (£4,200 ÷ 1000 sq m) x 200 = 840	**1,470** (total costs ÷ total floor area) x floor area of warehouse & storage dept (£4,200 ÷ 1000 sq m) x 350 = 1,470	**630** (total costs ÷ total floor area) x floor area of selling & distribution dept (£4,200 ÷ 1000 sq m) x 150 = 630
Cleaning of whole premises	**Floor area**	7,500	**2,250** (total costs ÷ total floor area) x floor area of assembly dept (£7,500 ÷ 1000 sq m) x 300 = 2,250	**1,500** (total costs ÷ total floor area) x floor area of finishing dept (£7,500 ÷ 1000 sq m) x 200 = 1,500	**2,625** (total costs ÷ total floor area) x floor area of warehouse & storage dept (£7,500 ÷ 1000 sq m) x 350 = 2,625	**1,125** (total costs ÷ total floor area) x floor area of selling & distribution dept (£7,500 ÷ 1000 sq m) x 150 = 1,125
Warehouse and storage costs	**Allocated**	9,400			**9,400** Allocated to this department only	
Total		41,500	12,150	9,300	16,855	3,195
Re-apportionment: Warehouse and storage			**6,742** (total cost ÷ total material requisitions) x material requisitions for assembly dept (£16,855 ÷ 1,500) x 600 = 6,742	**10,113** (total cost ÷ total material requisitions) x material requisitions for finishing dept (£16,855 ÷ 1,500) x 900 = 10,113	-16,855	
Re-apportionment: Selling and distribution			**1,598** total cost ÷ 2 = 1,598 rounded	**1,597** total cost ÷ 2 = 1,598 rounded down to equal total – # see note below		-3,195
Total		41,500	20,490	21,010		

Further explanations:

When your table is complete, you should be able to double check your figures.

The totals for each department after the initial apportionment should equal the total budgeted overheads. £12,150 + £9,300 + £16,855 + £3,195 = £41,500.

The totals for each of the production centres after re-apportionment should equal the total budgeted overheads. £20,490 + £21,010 = £41,500.

Note #: The total was rounded down in this calculation because the total of the re-apportioned amount needs to total the amount to be re-apportioned.

Task 5: (15 marks) answers

You have been provided with the following budgeted information.

	Department Muddle £	Department Huddle £
Budgeted Overheads	450,000	520,000
Actual Overheads	433,000	515,000
Budgeted Labour Hours	2,250	840
Actual Labour Hours	2,330	780
Budgeted Machine Hours	420	1,250
Actual Machine Hours	425	1,120

a) Calculate the budgeted overhead absorption rate for Department Muddle using labour hours, and for Department Huddle using machine hours. (7 marks)

	Department Muddle £	Department Huddle £
Budgeted overhead absorption rate OAR	**200** **Budgeted overheads ÷ budgeted labour hours. £450,000 ÷ 2,250 hours = 200**	**416** **Budgeted overheads ÷ budgeted machine hours. £520,000 ÷ 1,250 = 416**

b) Calculate the over or under absorption for each department. (7 marks)

	Overheads incurred £	Overheads absorbed £	Difference £	Under/over absorption
Department Muddle	**433,000** **Actual overheads taken from table above**	**466,000** **OAR x actual labour hours** **£200 x 2,330 hours =**	**33,000** **Difference between overheads incurred and overheads absorbed**	**Over-absorbed** **Overheads absorbed are higher than overheads incurred**
Department Huddle	**515,000** **Actual overheads taken from table above**	**465,920** **OAR x actual machine hours** **£416 x 1,120 = 465,920**	**49,080** **Difference between overheads incurred and overheads absorbed**	**Under-absorbed** **Overheads absorbed are lower than overheads incurred**

c) An under absorption of overheads will be ~~debited~~ / *credited* to the Statement of Profit or Loss. (delete as appropriate) (1 mark)

Explanation: This is debited to the SOPL because this is essentially an expense to the business as the overheads were not fully absorbed.

Task 6: (25 marks) answers

a) Using the following information, complete the table below to calculate the profit of the planned production of each product. Round your answers to the nearest whole £. (20 marks)

Budgeted units for Product AB1 are 5,000 units.

Budgeted units for Product AC2 are 25% more than AB1 and budgeted units for Product AD3 is 10% more than AC2.

The sale price per unit of AB1 is £6. The sale price of AC2 is 15% more than AB1. The sale price of AD3 is 20% more than AC2.

Variable costs per unit of AB1 is £1. Variable costs per unit for AC2 and AD3 is 10% more than AB1.

Fixed costs of £1,800 are to be shared between AB1, AC2 and AD3 in the ratio of 3:2:1.

	Product AB1	Product AC2	Product AD3
Budgeted Units	**5,000** Given in information above	**6,250** 5,000 add 25%. 5,000 x 1.25 = 6,250	**6,875** 6,250 add 10%. 6,250 x 1.10 = 6,875
Sales revenue £	**30,000** £6 each x 5,000 units = £30,000	**43,125** £6 add 15%. £6 x 1.15 = 6.90. £6.90 x 6,250 units = 43,125	**56,925** £6.90 add 20%. £6.90 x 1.20 = 8.28. £8.28 x 6,875 units = 56,925
Variable Costs £	**5,000** Variable cost per unit is £1 x 5,000 units = 5,000	**6,875** £1 add 10%. £1 x 1.10 = £1.10. £1.10 x 6,250 units = 6,875	**7,563** £1 add 10%. £1 x 1.10 = £1.10. £1.10 x 6,875 units = 7,562.50 so round up to 7,563
Contribution £	**25,000** Sales revenue less variable costs 30,000 − 5,000 = 25,000	**36,250** 43,125 − 6,875 = 36,250	**49,362** 56,925 − 7,563 = 49,362

Fixed Costs £	900	600	300
	Fixed costs ÷ 6 = 300 300 x 3 = 900 (# see explanation below)	Fixed costs ÷ 6 = 300 300 x 2 = 600	Fixed costs ÷ 6 = 300 300 x 1 = 300
Profit £	24,100	35,650	49,062
	Contribution less fixed costs 25,000 – 900 = 24,100	36,250 – 600 = 35,650	49,362 – 300 = 49,062

Explanation: # Ratio calculation:

The ratio for the sharing of the fixed costs is 3:2:1.

This is shared like this:

3 + 2 + 1 = 6 parts

£1,800 ÷ 6 parts = £300

3 parts for AB1 = £900

2 parts for AC2 = £600

1 part for AD3 = £300

b) Your friend works for a rival company and has asked for details about his budget. Do you release this information? Explain your answer. (5 marks)

Suggested answer: (remember that your answer will differ from mine, but make sure you have the main points explained – underlined below)

I cannot release this information to my friend as this information is confidential. It would be a breach of my fundamental ethical principle of confidentiality, as well as a possible breach of Data Protection legislation or GDPR. I would politely tell my friend that I can't give her this information. I would report this request to my manager.

Task 7: (16 marks) answers

Using the information below, complete the table to calculate the total products we can produce based on the limiting factor.

Product	Total labour hours	Budgeted production levels	Total contribution £
Rum Tum	125	250	750
Bing Bong	225	300	630
Lim Lam	120	200	640

Total fixed costs are £900, and this is to be shared equally between the product ranges.

Due to Covid, we have a limited number of production staff available, so the total labour hours available is 400.

Complete the following table. Round your answers to two decimal places.

	Rum Tum	Bing Bong	Lim Lam	Total
Contribution per Unit £	**3** Total contribution ÷ budgeted production 750 ÷ 250 = 3	**2.10** 630 ÷ 300 = 2.10	**3.20** 640 ÷ 200 = 3.20	**8.30** 3 + 2.10 + 3.20 = 8.30
Contribution per labour hour £	**6** Total contribution ÷ total labour hours 750 ÷ 125 = 6	**2.80** 630 ÷225 = 2.8	**5.33** 640 ÷120 = 5.33	**14.13**
Ranking	**1** Highest contribution per limiting factor – labour hour	**3**	**2**	
Total labour hours available				**400**
Labour hours allocated	**125** Hours needed for the budgeted production	**155** Balance of hours available for production	**120** Hours needed for the budgeted production	**400**

Units to Produce	250	207	200	657
	Budgeted production level	300 ÷ 225 hours = 1.33333 (leave answer in your calculator) x 155 hours = 207 rounded	Budgeted production	
Total Contribution	750	435	640	1,825
	Contribution per unit x production level £3 x 250 = 750	£2.10 x 207 = 435 rounded	£3.20 x 200 = 640	
Less Fixed Costs	300	300	300	900
	£900 shared equally £900 ÷ 3 = 300			
Profit	450	135	340	925
	Contribution – fixed costs 750 – 300 = 450	435 - 300 = 135 rounded	640 – 300 = 340	1,825 – 900 = 925 Check: 450 + 135 + 340 = 925

Task 8: (16 marks) answers

Identify the correct cost classification for each of the following. Choose from *fixed, variable, semi-variable and stepped.*

a) Cost classification 1: (4 marks)

Units	Cost per unit
2,000	£16.00
3,000	£14.00
5,000	£12.40
8,000	£11.50

Cost classification – *fixed / variable (semi-variable)/ stepped*

Explanation:

The cost per unit varies with the quantity so this is not a variable cost.

Remember that variable means that the cost remains constant per unit.

The cost per unit multiplied by the number of units is different for each quantity.

2,000 units x £16 = £32,000

3,000 units x £14 = £42,000

5,000 units x £12.40 = £62,000

8,000 units x £11.50 = £92,000

This is not fixed because a fixed cost, such as rent, remains the same despite the quantity produced.

Neither is this stepped because the total cost for each quantity is different at each level.

This one must, therefore, be a semi-variable cost.

b) Calculate the total cost for 10,000 units. (4 marks)

£112,000
High low method is used to separate fixed and variable costs and we need
to do this first to be able to calculate the total cost for 10,000 units.
Highest cost £92,000 – lowest cost £32,000 = £60,000
Highest units 8,000 – lowest units 2,000 = 6,000
Divide the cost by the units to get the variable cost per unit:
£60,000 ÷ 6,000 units = £10
This is the variable cost per unit.
For the fixed cost we go back to the highest (or lowest) units:
8,000 units x £10 (variable cost per unit) = £80,000
Total cost less variable cost = fixed cost
£92,000 - £80,000 = £12,000.
This is the fixed cost.
We now have a variable cost per unit of £10 and a fixed cost of £12,000
Cost for 10,000 units:
Variable cost = £10 x 10,000 units = £100,000
Fixed cost = £12,000
Total cost = £112,000

c) Cost classification 2: (4 marks)

Units	Total cost
2,000	£18,000
3,000	£27,000
5,000	£45,000
8,000	£72,000

Cost classification – *fixed* / *variable* / *semi-variable* / *stepped*

Explanation:

The total cost varies with the quantity, so this is not a fixed cost, such as rent.

The cost per unit is the same for each quantity.

£18,000 ÷ 2,000 units = £9

£27,000 ÷ 3,000 units = £9

£45,000 ÷ 5,000 units = £9

£72,000 ÷ 8,000 units = £9

As the cost per unit remains the same, this is a variable cost. This varies with how many are made. 1 unit is £9, 2 units are £18 etc.

d) Calculate the total cost for 10,000 units. (4 marks)

£90,000
This is a variable cost, and we know the variable cost per unit is £9.
£9 x 10,000 units = £90,000
Total cost for 10,000 units = £90,000

Task 9: (16 marks) answers

a) You have been asked to prepare the flexed budget and then compare your new budget with the actual results. Complete the following table. (12 marks)

Adverse variances should be shown with a minus sign or brackets.

Round your answers to the nearest whole £.

	Budget	Flexed Budget	Actual	Variance
Units	60,000	56,000	56,000	
	£	£	£	£
Sales revenue	1,380,000	**1,288,000** £1,380,000 ÷ 60,000 units = £23 £23 x 56,000 units = £1,288,000	1,340,000	**52,000** Actual sales income was higher than the flexed budget, so this is a favourable variance.
Less costs				
Manufacturing costs	252,000	**235,200** £252,000 ÷ 60,000 units = £4.20 £4.20 x 56,000 units = £235,200	230,000	**5,200** Actual costs were lower than the flexed budget, so this is a favourable variance.
Delivery costs	180,000	**168,000** £180,000 ÷ 60,000 units = £3 £3 x 56,000 units = £168,000	172,000	**-4000** Actual costs were higher than the flexed budget, so this is an adverse variance.
Fixed overheads	138,000	**138,000** Fixed should remain fixed as per the original budget	130,500	**7,500** Actual costs were lower than the flexed budget, so this is a favourable variance.
Profit	810,000	**746,800** £1,288,000 – £235,200 - £168,000 - £138,000 = £746,800	807,500	**60,700** Actual profit was higher than the flexed budget, so this is a favourable variance.

b) Explain a possible reason for the sales revenue variance. (4 marks)

Suggested answer:

Note that your answer will be worded different to mine but ensure that you have the main point (under-lined below).

The actual sales income was much higher than the flexed budget. The reason for this is not the number of units sold, as we used the same sales figure of 56,000 units.

However, the actual total sales revenue was higher, so this must be due to a <u>rise in the sales price</u>.

The budget was to sell the units at £23 each (£1,288,000 ÷ 56,000 units).

The actual sales were at an average price of £23.93 each rounded (£1,340,000 ÷ 56,000) units).

Task 10: (20 marks) answers

The following information has been received and you have been asked to comment on the proposals:

Appraisal	Notes	Company Policy	Project Results
Payback Period		Accept if 3.5 years or less	4 years
Net Present Value NPV	Discount at 12% cost of capital	Accept if positive	£30,000 +
Internal Rate of Return	Discount at 12% cost of capital	Must exceed cost of capital	11%

Evaluate this information and suggest to the manager whether to accept the proposed project.

Appraisal method	Recommendation
Payback period	**Reject as payback period is longer than company policy.** This is the time it will take for the company to get their initial investment back and they want this back within 3.5 years.
NPV	**Accept as NPV is positive** This is the value of the project, so a positive number is very important. A negative number would imply a loss on the project.
IRR	**Reject as IRR does not exceed the cost of capital.** The cost of capital is 12% and the project results show only 11%.
Overall	**Accept based on the most important criteria.** The most important criteria is the net present value, NPV.

Marks sheet:

Task	Available marks	Your marks - first attempt	Your marks – second attempt	Notes
1	16			
2a	4			
2b	4			
2c	4			
2d	4			
3a	10			
3b	2			
4	18			
5a	7			
5b	7			
5c	1			
6a	20			
6b	5			
7	16			
8a	4			
8b	4			
8c	4			
8d	4			
9a	12			
9b	4			
10	20			
Total	170			

To work out your mark as a percentage:

(Your marks ÷ total marks available) x 100

Example: (136 marks ÷ 170 marks) x 100 = 80%

AAT Level 3 Management Accounting: Costing

Practice Assessment 2

By

Teresa Clarke FMAAT

This practice assessment has been designed and written to be like the real AAT Level 3 Management Accounting: Costing exam. It includes a similar mark scheme so you can work out your percentage pass rate too.

Answers are shown on page 56 onwards. A marks sheet is included at the back of this assessment for you to record your marks. You need 70% to pass this exam.

NOTE:

Unlike other practice assessments, I have shown workings and given explanations to help you understand the answers. This will help you to understand any errors you make.

Time allowed – 2 hours 30 minutes

Task 1: (16 marks)

You have been provided with the following information about raw materials purchased by your organisation.

Date of Purchase	Number of Units	Cost per Unit £	Total Cost £
1 August 2021	620	2.10	1,302
3 August 2021	380	2.15	817
6 August 2021	320	2.40	768

An issue was made from stores to the production department on 7 August 2021 of 450 units.

a) Complete the table below. Round your answers to two decimal places. (12 marks)

	Cost
FIFO issue	
LIFO issue	
FIFO balance	
LIFO balance	

Workings:

b) First in first out (FIFO) means that the value of the closing inventory is based on the latest purchase price. (4 marks) *True / False*

Task 2: (16 marks)

Shanaz uses the following codes in her accounting payroll system.

Ledger	Code
Wages control account	4500
Direct production costs	5000
Operating overheads	5500
Non-operating overheads	6000

Using these codes complete the tables below.

a) Paid wages of production employees. 300 hours at £10.50 per hour. (4 marks)

	Code	£
Debit		
Credit		

b) Paid wages of warehouse employees. £500 plus overtime of £150. (4 marks)

	Code	£
Debit		
Credit		

c) Paid wages of office staff. 3 employees at £420 each. (4 marks)

	Code	£
Debit		
Credit		

d) Paid wages of packaging employees. Total £600. (4 marks)

	Code	£
Debit		
Credit		

Task 3: (12 marks)

Production workers are paid at a basic rate of £12 per hour.

There are two overtime rates:

Overtime rate 1 is paid at basic pay plus 20%.

Overtime rate 2 is paid at basic pay plus 30%.

The team are expected to manufacture 6 units per hour.

A bonus of £1.50 per unit is paid for any units manufactured in excess of the target.

There are 10 people in the production team.

The team worked 96 hours on Monday and manufactured 640 units.

a) Calculate the total labour cost for the production team on Monday by completing the table below. Round your answers to 2 decimal places. (10 marks)

Labour cost	Hours worked	Amount due £
Basic pay	80	
Overtime rate 1	10	
Overtime rate 2	6	
Total cost before bonus		
Bonus pay		
Total wages cost including team bonus		

44

b) Calculate the labour cost per production employee for Monday. Round
   your answer to 2 decimal places. (2 marks)

Task 4: (18 marks)

Ulita M Ltd has the following budgeted overheads for the year.

Rent and rates	£55,000
Power for production machinery	£14,000
Depreciation of machinery	£18,000
Light and heat	£31,000
Indirect labour costs:	
Maintenance	£12,000
Administration	£24,000

You have been provided with the following information about the cost centres.

Basis	Production Centre A	Production Centre B	Maintenance	Administration
Floor area m²	4,000	5,000	100	900
Carrying value of machinery £	400,000	800,000	0	0
Production machinery power usage KwH)	12,000	13,000	0	0
Time spent maintaining production machinery	500	1,500	0	0

Complete the table below, allocating and apportioning the overheads over all four cost centres.

Re-apportion the maintenance centre costs using the time spend maintaining production machinery.
Re-apportion administration centre costs equally between the production centres.

Round your answers to the nearest whole £.

Overhead	Basis of allocation or apportion-ment £	Total £	Production centre 1 £	Production centre 2 £	Maintenance £	Administra-tion £
Rent and rates						
Power for production machinery						
Depreciation of machinery						
Light and heat						
Indirect labour						
Total						
Re-apportionment: Maintenance costs						
Re-apportionment: Administration costs						
Total						

Task 5: (15 marks)

You have been provided with the following budgeted information.

	Manufacturing £	Assembly £
Budgeted Overheads	36,540	24,960
Actual Overheads	38,000	30,000
Budgeted Labour Hours	180	95
Actual Labour Hours	170	110
Budgeted Machine Hours	86	160
Actual Machine Hours	88	195

a) Calculate the budgeted overhead absorption rate for the manufacturing department using labour hours, and for the assembly department using machine hours. (7 marks)

	Manufacturing £	Assembly £
Budgeted overhead absorption rate OAR		

b) Calculate the over or under absorption for the assembly department. (5 marks)

Over-absorbed / under-absorbed by £ [   ]

c) If the value of the actual overheads exceeds the overheads absorbed for the quarter, this will mean that the business has
over-absorbed / under-absorbed
the overheads. (3 marks)

Task 6: (25 marks)

You have been provided with the following information about a new product, the KC1. The KC1 will be produced in batches of 2,500.

New product KC1	Costs per batch £
Direct materials	11,500
Direct labour	8,125
Variable overheads	7,500
Fixed production overheads	13,000
Administration and selling overheads	9,000
Total costs	49,125

a) Calculate the prime cost per batch of the KC1. (3 marks)

b) Calculate the marginal cost per batch of the KC1. (3 marks)

c) Calculate the full absorption cost per batch of the KC1. (3 marks)

d) Calculate the prime cost of one unit of the KC1. (3 marks)

e) Calculate the marginal cost of one unit of the KC1. (3 marks)

f) Calculate the full absorption cost of one unit of the KC1. (3 marks)

g) Which one of the following is an example of a direct cost? (2 marks)

Materials used to repair production machinery.	
Materials used for a special order of the KC1.	
Labour used to repair the production machinery.	

h) Your manager has asked you to reduce the material cost of the product with no explanation, thereby increasing the budgeted profit. Which one of the following actions should you take? (5 marks)

Change the material cost without question as your manager knows best.	
Agree to change the figures, but then leave them as they were making no changes.	
Ask your manager for an explanation before you consider making any changes.	
Show the figures to a friend who is an accountant in another organisation and ask for their advice on what to do.	

Task 7: (16 marks)

Beth has an ice cream selling business. She sells her ice creams at £3 each. The total variable cost per ice cream is £1.20. Her total fixed costs for the month of July are £600.

a) Calculate the budgeted breakeven, in units, for Beth's ice creams.
   Tip: Remember to round up to the nearest whole unit. (4 marks)

	units

b) Calculate the budgeted breakeven, in £, for Beth's ice creams. (3 marks)

£	

c) Beth plans to sell 1,000 ice creams in July. Calculate Beth's margin of safety in units. (3 marks)

	Units

d) Calculate the margin of safety as a percentage of the planned sales. (3 marks)

	%

e) Beth wishes to make a profit of £800. How many units must she sell to achieve this target profit? (3 marks)

	Units

Task 8: (16 marks)

Complete the following table by choosing the correct description for each of the four types of cost.

Cost	Description
Total cost	
Fixed cost	
Variable cost	
Semi variable cost	
Stepped cost	

Options:

1	Made up of fixed and variable costs
2	Fixed for a certain level of production only
3	Increases in total as volume increases
4	Made up of variable and semi-variable costs
5	Decreases per unit as volume increases
6	Made up of all costs added together
7	Total cost decreases as volume increases
8	Made up of stepped and variable costs

Task 9: (16 marks)

a) Complete the table below to show the new flexed budget and the variances when compared with the actual figures. (12 marks)

Adverse variances should be shown with minus signs.

Round your answers to the nearest whole £.

	Original Budget	Flexed Budget	Actual	Variance
Number of units	13,000		14,500	
	£	£	£	£
Sales revenue	127,400		138,000	
Less costs				
Direct materials	27,300		19,000	
Direct labour	22,100		26,000	
Fixed overheads	32,000		33,000	
Profit from operations	46,000		60,000	

b) Identify which variance had the biggest impact on the profit. (4 marks)

Task 10: (20 marks)

Tatley Manufacturing is considering three possible investments. They are very interested in the return on capital but have also asked you to comment on the payback period.

Appraisal method	Investment A	Investment B	Investment C
Payback period (years)	3.8	3.1	5.7
Net present value (£)	28,000	-31,000	33,000

a) Based on the payback period, which investment would you recommend? (5 marks)

Investment A	
Investment B	
Investment C	

b) Based on the net present value, which investment would you recommend? (5 marks)

Investment A	
Investment B	
Investment C	

c) Using your answers to a) and b) and the information above, which investment would you recommend to Tatley Manufacturing? (5 marks)

Investment A	
Investment B	
Investment C	

d) Which of the following describes the internal rate of return? (5 marks)

The time it takes for a business to get its initial investment back.	
The discount rate that gives a net present value of zero.	
The value of the project after taking into account the cost of capital.	

Answers

Answers are shown in bold.

Workings and explanations are included to help you understand the answers.

Task 1: (16 marks) answers

You have been provided with the following information about raw materials purchased by your organisation.

Date of Purchase	Number of Units	Cost per Unit £	Total Cost £
1 August 2021	620	2.10	1,302
3 August 2021	380	2.15	817
6 August 2021	320	2.40	768

An issue was made from stores to the production department on 7 August 2021 of 450 units.

a) Complete the table below. Round your answers to two decimal places. (12 marks)

	Cost
FIFO issue	**£945.00** 450 units at £2.10 = £945
LIFO issue	**£1,047.50** 320 units at £2.40 = £768 130 units at £2.15 = £279.50 Total 450 units = £1,047.50
FIFO balance	**£1,942.00** Total balance of £1,302 + £817 + £768 = £2,887 £2,887 less issue £945 = £1,942
LIFO balance	**£1,839.50** Total balance of £2,887 less issue £1,047.52 = £1,839.50

b) First in first out (FIFO) means that the value of the closing inventory is based on the latest purchase price. (4 marks) *True* / False

Explanation: The FIFO method issues inventory at the oldest inventory first, so the closing inventory is valued at the latest purchase price.

Task 2: (16 marks) answers

Shanaz uses the following codes in her accounting payroll system.

Ledger	Code
Wages control account	4500
Direct production costs	5000
Operating overheads	5500
Non-operating overheads	6000

Using these codes complete the tables below.

a) Paid wages of production employees. 300 hours at £10.50 per hour.
(4 marks)

	Code	£
Debit	5000	3,150
Credit	4500	3,150

Explanation: The wages control is credited with the amount owed to the employee and the wages expense, in this case production costs, is debited as the expense.

b) Paid wages of warehouse employees. £500 plus overtime of £150.
(4 marks)

	Code	£
Debit	5500	650
Credit	4500	650

Explanation: The wages control is credited with the amount owed to the employee and the wages expense, in this case operating overheads, is debited as the expense. This is the operating overheads cost code as these are employees working as part of the manufacturing team.

Tip: Think of the factory building as operating overheads and the office as non-operating overheads.

c) Paid wages of office staff. 3 employees at £420 each. (4 marks)

	Code	£
Debit	6000	1,260
Credit	4500	1,260

Explanation: The wages control is credited with the amount owed to the employee and the wages expense, in this case non-operating overheads, is debited as the expense. These are employees working in the office and not part of the manufacturing process.

d) Paid wages of packaging employees. Total £600. (4 marks)

	Code	£
Debit	5500	600
Credit	4500	600

Explanation: The wages control is credited with the amount owed to the employee and the wages expense, in this case operating overheads, is debited as the expense. Operating overheads is used as these are employees working as part of the manufacturing team.

Task 3: (12 marks) answers

Production workers are paid at a basic rate of £12 per hour.

There are two overtime rates:

Overtime rate 1 is paid at basic pay plus 20%.

Overtime rate 2 is paid at basic pay plus 30%.

The team are expected to manufacture 6 units per hour.

A bonus of £1.50 per unit is paid for any units manufactured in excess of the target.

There are 10 people in the production team.

The team worked 96 hours on Monday and manufactured 640 units.

a) Calculate the total labour cost for the production team on Monday by completing the table below. Round your answers to 2 decimal places. (10 marks)

Labour cost	Hours worked	Amount due £
Basic pay	80	**960.00** 80 hours x £12 per hour = 960.00
Overtime rate 1	10	**144.00** 10 hours x (£12 x 120%) = 144.00
Overtime rate 2	6	**93.60** 6 hours x (£12 x 1.3) = 93.60
Total cost before bonus		**1,197.60** 960.00 + 144.00 + 93.60 = 1,197.60
Bonus pay		**96.00** Target is 6 units per hour. Total hours worked was 96. 96 hours x 6 units = 576. Units produced was 640. 640 units – 576 = 64 units in excess of target. 64 x £1.50 (bonus rate) = 96
Total wages cost including team bonus		**1,293.60** 1,197.60 + 96 = 1,293.60

b) Calculate the labour cost per production employee for Monday. Round your answer to 2 decimal places. (2 marks)

> **Total labour cost was £1,293.60.**
> **There were 10 employees.**
> **£1,293.60 ÷ 10 employees = <u>£129.36</u>**

Task 4: (18 marks) answers

Ulita M Ltd has the following budgeted overheads for the year.

Rent and rates	£55,000
Power for production machinery	£14,000
Depreciation of machinery	£18,000
Light and heat	£31,000
Indirect labour costs:	
Maintenance	£12,000
Administration	£24,000

You have been provided with the following information about the cost centres.

Basis	Production Centre A	Production Centre B	Maintenance	Administration
Floor area m²	4,000	5,000	100	900
Carrying value of machinery £	400,000	800,000	0	0
Production machinery power usage KwH)	12,000	13,000	0	0
Time spent maintaining production machinery	500	1,500	0	0

Complete the table below, allocating and apportioning the overheads over all four cost centres.

Re-apportion the maintenance centre costs using the time spend maintaining production machinery.
Re-apportion administration centre costs equally between the production centres.

Round your answers to the nearest whole £.

Overhead	Basis of allocation or apportionment £	Total £	Production centre 1 £	Production centre 2 £	Maintenance £	Administration £
Rent and rates	**Floor area**	**55,000**	**22,000** (55,000 ÷ total floor area 10,000) x cost centre floor area 4,000 = 22,000	**27,500** (55,000 ÷ total floor area 10,000) x cost centre floor area 5,000 = 27,500	**550** (55,000 ÷ total floor area 10,000) x cost centre floor area 100 = 550	**4,950** (55,000 ÷ total floor area 10,000) x cost centre floor area 900 = 4,950
Power for production machinery	**Production machinery power usage**	**14,000**	**6,720** (14,000 ÷ total power usage 25,000) x cost centre power usage 12,000 = 6,720	**7,280** (14,000 ÷ total power usage 25,000) x cost centre power usage 13,000 = 7,280	**0**	**0**
Depreciation of machinery	**Carrying value of machinery**	**18,000**	**6,000** (18,000 ÷ total carrying value 1,200,000) x cost centre carrying value 400,000 = 6,000	**12,000** (18,000 ÷ total carrying value 1,200,000) x cost centre carrying value 800,000 = 12,000	**0**	**0**
Light and heat	**Floor area**	**31,000**	**12,400** (31,000 ÷ total floor area 10,000) x cost centre floor area 4,000 = 12,400	**15,500** (31,000 ÷ total floor area 10,000) x cost centre floor area 5,000 = 15,500	**310** (31,000 ÷ total floor area 10,000) x cost centre floor area 100 = 310	**2,790** (31,000 ÷ total floor area 10,000) x cost centre floor area 900 = 2,790
Indirect labour	**Allocated**	**36,000**	**0**	**0**	**12,000** The question told you the allocated cost centre for this.	**24,000** The question told you the allocated cost centre for this.

Total		154,000 Total of all costs	47,120 Total for this cost centre	62,280 Total for this cost centre	12,860 Total for this cost centre	31,740 Total for this cost centre
Re-apportionment: maintenance costs	**Time spent maintaining machinery**		**3,215** (12,860 ÷ total maintenance hours 2,000) x cost centre maintenance hours 500 = 3,215	**9,645** (12,860 ÷ total maintenance hours 2,000) x cost centre maintenance hours 1500 = 9,645	**-12,860**	
Re-apportionment: administration costs			**15,870** 31,740 ÷ 2 = 15,870	**15,870** 31,740 ÷ 2 = 15,870		**-31,740**
Total		154,000	**66,205** 47,120 + 3,215 + 15,870 = 66,205	**87,795** 62,280 + 9,645 + 15,870 = 87,795		

Remember to cross check your apportioned costs by checking that the apportioned amounts equal the total for each overhead. Check that the cost centre totals equal the total overheads. Check that the final re-apportioned overheads for each production centre equal the total overheads.

Task 5: (15 marks) answers

You have been provided with the following budgeted information.

	Manufacturing £	Assembly £
Budgeted Overheads	36,540	24,960
Actual Overheads	38,000	30,000
Budgeted Labour Hours	180	95
Actual Labour Hours	170	110
Budgeted Machine Hours	86	160
Actual Machine Hours	88	195

a) Calculate the budgeted overhead absorption rate for the manufacturing department using labour hours, and for the assembly department using machine hours. (7 marks)

	Manufacturing £	Assembly £
Budgeted overhead absorption rate OAR	**203** Budgeted overheads ÷ budgeted labour hours 36,540 / 180 = 203	**156** Budgeted overheads ÷ budgeted machine hours 24,960 / 160 = 156

b) Calculate the over or under absorption for the assembly department. (5 marks)

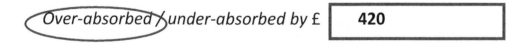 Over-absorbed / under-absorbed by £ | **420**

Workings: Budgeted overhead absorption rate of £156 multiplied by actual machine hours 195 = £30,420.

Actual overheads incurred £30,000.

Difference between overheads absorbed and actual overheads is £420.

The overheads absorbed are £420 higher than the actual overheads incurred, so the overheads have been over-absorbed.

c) If the value of the actual overheads exceeds the overheads absorbed for the quarter, this will mean that the business has
   *over-absorbed / **under-absorbed***
   the overheads.   (3 marks)

Explanation: If the overheads absorbed are higher than the actual overheads, then this is an over-absorption.

If actual overheads are higher than absorbed overheads, then this is an under-absorption.

Task 6: (25 marks) answers

You have been provided with the following information about a new product, the KC1. The KC1 will be produced in batches of 2,500.

New product KC1	Costs per batch £
Direct materials	11,500
Direct labour	8,125
Variable overheads	7,500
Fixed production overheads	13,000
Administration and selling overheads	9,000
Total costs	49,125

a) Calculate the prime cost per batch of the KC1. (3 marks)

> **£19,625**
> **Direct materials + direct labour**
> **11,500 + 8,125 = 19,625**

b) Calculate the marginal cost per batch of the KC1. (3 marks)

> **£27,125**
> **Prime cost + variable costs**
> **19,625 + 7,500 = 27,125**

c) Calculate the full absorption cost per batch of the KC1. (3 marks)

> **£40,125**
> **Marginal cost + fixed production overheads**
> **NEVER INCLUDE THE NON-PRODUCTION OVERHEADS**
> **27,125 + 13,000 = 40,125**

d) Calculate the prime cost of one unit of the KC1. (3 marks)

> **£7.85**
> **Prime cost ÷ number of units in batch**
> **19,625 ÷ 2,500 units = 7.85**

e) Calculate the marginal cost of one unit of the KC1. (3 marks)

> **£10.85**
> 27,125 ÷ 2,500 units = 10.85

f) Calculate the full absorption cost of one unit of the KC1. (3 marks)

> **£16.05**
> 40,125 ÷ 2,500 units = 16.05

g) Which one of the following is an example of a direct cost? (2 marks)

Materials used to repair production machinery.	
Materials used for a special order of the KC1.	√
Labour used to repair the production machinery.	

Explanation: Direct costs are materials or labour which are directly used to produce a unit, for example the wood to make a table or the carpenter's time to make the table. The materials used to repair the machinery is not part of the manufacturing process. The labour used to repair the machinery is not part of the manufacturing process. The materials used for a special order are materials that are directly used to make the product.

h) Your manager has asked you to reduce the material cost of the product with no explanation, thereby increasing the budgeted profit. Which one of the following actions should you take? (5 marks)

Change the material cost without question as your manager knows best.	
Agree to change the figures, but then leave them as they were making no changes.	
Ask your manager for an explanation before you consider making any changes.	**√**
Show the figures to a friend who is an accountant in another organisation and ask for their advice on what to do.	

Explanation: You should not breach your professional competence and due care by using figures that you have not checked are correct. You should always question something that you are unsure of.
You would not change the cost without question.
You would not agree to make changes and then leave them as they are.
You would not show the figures to your friend as they would breach your professional ethical principle of confidentiality.
You should ask your manager to explain why he wants the figures changed to ensure that you are doing the correct thing.

Task 7: (16 marks) answers

Beth has an ice cream selling business. She sells her ice creams at £3 each. The total variable cost per ice cream is £1.20. Her total fixed costs for the month of July are £600.

a) Calculate the budgeted breakeven, in units, for Beth's ice creams.
   Tip: Remember to round up to the nearest whole unit. (4 marks)

> **334 units**
> Breakeven = total fixed costs ÷ contribution per unit
> Contribution is sales price - variable costs.
> Total fixed costs of £600
> Sale price £3 – variable costs £1.20
> £600 ÷ £1.80 = 333.33 rounded up to 334 units

b) Calculate the budgeted breakeven, in £, for Beth's ice creams. (3 marks)

> **£1,002**
> Breakeven in £ is the same as breakeven in revenue.
> Breakeven units x sales price per unit.
> 334 units x £3 each = 1,002

c) Beth plans to sell 1,000 ice creams in July. Calculate Beth's margin of safety in units. (3 marks)

> **666 units**
> Margin of safety is the difference between the planned sales and the breakeven point in units.
> 1,000 units – 334 units = 666 units

d) Calculate the margin of safety as a percentage of the planned sales. (3 marks)

> **66.6%**
> Margin of safety as a percentage of sales is calculated by taking the margin of safety and dividing this by the planned sales, then multiplying your answer by 100 to turn it into a percentage.
> $\frac{666}{1,000}$ x 100
> Calculate by dividing 666 by 1,000 first, then leave your answer in your calculator and multiply by 100.
> 66.6%

e) Beth wishes to make a profit of £800. How many units must she sell to achieve this target profit? (3 marks)

778 units
Target profit is calculated in a similar way to breakeven point, but with the added target profit.
<u>Total fixed costs + target profit</u>
Contribution per unit (sales price - variable costs)
<u>600 + 800</u>
1.80
To calculate: 600 + 800 = 1,400
1,400 ÷ 1.80 = 777.777 rounded up to the nearest whole unit 778.

Task 8: (16 marks) answers

Complete the following table by choosing the correct description for each of the four types of cost.

Cost	Description
Total cost	**6** Total costs is all of the costs added together.
Fixed cost	**5** Fixed costs decrease per unit as the volume increases. For example, rent of £1,000 ÷ 10 units = £100 each. Rent of £1,000 ÷ 200 units = £5 each. The cost per unit has decreased as the volume has increased.
Variable cost	**3** This increases in total as volume increases. One unit may cost £1, two units would cost £2 and 200 units would cost £200. So the total cost has increased as the volume has increased.
Semi variable cost	**1** This is made of a fixed element and a variable cost per unit.
Stepped cost	**2** This is fixed for a certain level of production and then increases in a step. For example, we may rent a storage unit for up to 1,000 units, but when we have 1,001 units to store, we will need a second warehouse.

Options:

1	Made up of fixed and variable costs
2	Fixed for a certain level of production only
3	Increases in total as volume increases
4	Made up of variable and semi-variable costs
5	Decreases per unit as volume increases
6	Made up of all costs added together
7	Total cost decreases as volume increases
8	Made up of stepped and variable costs

Task 9: (16 marks) answers

a) Complete the table below to show the new flexed budget and the variances when compared with the actual figures. (12 marks)

Adverse variances should be shown with minus signs.

Round your answers to the nearest whole £.

	Original Budget	Flexed Budget	Actual	Variance
Number of Units	13,000	**14,500** This will always need to match the actual number of units	14,500	
	£	£	£	£
Sales revenue	127,400	**142,100** (Total sales revenue ÷ original units) x flexed budget units (127,400 ÷ 13,000) x 14,500 = 142,100	138,000	**-4,100** The actual sales revenue is lower than the budget, so this is an adverse variance.
Less costs				
Direct materials	27,300	**30,450** (Total direct materials cost ÷ original units) x flexed budget units (27,300 ÷ 13,000) x 14,500 = 30,450	19,000	**11,450** The actual cost of materials is lower than the budget, so this is a favourable variance.
Direct labour	22,100	**24,650** (Total direct labour cost ÷ original units) x flexed budget units (22,100 ÷ 13,000) x 14,500 = 24,650	26,000	**-1,350** The actual cost of labour is higher than the budget, so this is an adverse variance.
Fixed overheads	32,000	**32,000** Fixed overheads remain fixed in the flexed budget	33,000	**-1,000** The actual fixed overheads are higher than the budget, so this is an adverse variance.
Profit from operations	46,000	**55,000** Sales revenue – all costs	60,000	**5,000** The actual profit is higher than the budgeted profit, so this is a favourable variance.

b) Identify which variance had the biggest impact on the difference in the profit. (4 marks)

> **Direct materials**
> This was the highest variance, so this had the biggest impact on profit.

Task 10: (20 marks) answers

Tatley Manufacturing is considering three possible investments. They are very interested in the return on capital but have also asked you to comment on the payback period.

Appraisal method	Investment A	Investment B	Investment C
Payback period (years)	3.8	3.1	5.7
Net present value (£)	28,000	-31,000	33,000

a) Based on the payback period, which investment would you recommend? (5 marks)

Investment A	
Investment B	√
Investment C	

Explanation: The investment with the shortest payback period means that the initial investment will be returned quicker.

b) Based on the net present value, which investment would you recommend? (5 marks)

Investment A	
Investment B	
Investment C	√

Explanation: The investment with the highest, positive figure means that it is the investment with the best return on capital. It earns the business the most money. A negative figure is not good as this shows that the investment will give an overall loss.

c) Using your answers to a) and b) and the information provided, which investment would you recommend to Tatley Manufacturing? (5 marks)

Investment A	
Investment B	
Investment C	√

Explanation: This investment has the longest payback period, but as the return on investment is the main interest of the business, this investment gives the highest return, so should be recommended.

d) Which of the following describes the internal rate of return? (5 marks)

The time it takes for a business to get its initial investment back.	
The discount rate that gives a net present value of zero.	√
The value of the project after taking into account the cost of capital.	

Explanation: The first one describes the payback period, the third describes the net present value. The discount rate giving a return of zero is the internal rate of return, or the rate at which there is no profit or loss.

Marks sheet:

Task	Available marks	Your marks - first attempt	Your marks – second attempt	Notes
1a	12			
1b	4			
2a	4			
2b	4			
2c	4			
2d	4			
3a	10			
3b	2			
4	18			
5a	7			
5b	5			
5c	3			
6a	3			
6b	3			
6c	3			
6d	3			
6e	3			
6f	3			
6g	2			
6h	5			
7a	4			
7b	3			
7c	3			
7d	3			
7e	3			
8	16			
9a	12			
9b	4			

10a	5			
10b	5			
10c	5			
10d	5			
Total	170			

To work out your mark as a percentage:

(Your marks ÷ total marks available) x 100

Example: (136 marks ÷ 170 marks) x 100 = 80%

Printed in Great Britain
by Amazon

46124851R00044